How To Get A Job Online

A step by step guide to creating an online plan and resume

By Craig Britland

First Edition, 2016

Table of Contents

Introduction

Welcome to the Internet Age

Getting the right job can be one of the hardest and most stressful challenges you will ever face in your life. I learned this hard truth through my own experience of having to re-invent myself in the middle of the Great Recession. Fast forward to the present and I now find myself working as a career coach and applying the lessons I learned with my clients. I hope this workbook will serve and benefit you and your family. Good luck!

Welcome to the Internet Age! With all the benefits of modern technology, the work of finding and getting a job has changed dramatically. Whether you are entry-level, mid-career, or retired, the information included in this workbook will help you tailor your job search to today's market. As a volunteer career coach, I use this workbook to walk my clients through the process of planning and executing a winning job search strategy. The book is written in a workbook format so you can read it beginning to end, or start at any section for a specific phase of your job search. This is geared towards action; creating a winning plan and then executing it. It includes:

- How to create a plan and target your job search
- Instructions and fill-in tables to help you perform an accurate self-assessment
- A step by step method to create a winning resume
- Sample resume
- Sample letters
- Daily, weekly and monthly checklists to help you stay on track
- Blank notes pages to document your thoughts and ideas

You may be wondering if it is worth investing your time to read this material. With that in mind, I have tried to condense the lessons learned from over twenty years of work history at Intel, IHG, small companies and start-ups. In addition, I have used this same formula for both white and blue collar job seekers. To put it into perspective, I spent over seven thousand dollars for career coaching during the Great Recession, and this book contains more useful information than I received from that service. Is it worth it? You bet!

If you feel that you need more help or support, counseling services are available at: http://www.HowToGetAnOnlineJob.com.

How Things Are

In this section we will discuss how large, medium and small companies typically approach the candidate search. These are generalizations based upon my own experience. They may not represent how every company will approach the hiring process.

Large Corporations

Large corporations can be defined as Fortune 500 companies. Fortune Magazine ranks this list of the top five hundred US companies by fiscal revenue. Large corporations have massive human resource (HR) databases designed for managing and hiring employees. Since these companies have hundreds or thousands of available jobs, they receive hundreds and thousands of resumes each week. When an applicant applies to a specific job, an applicant profile is created which includes the targeted resume the candidate assigns to that application. Some databases allow applicants to upload multiple resumes per profile and other companies limit the applicant to one resume. Most resumes are not initially viewed by a person, but are instead stored in the database until a recruiter, HR manager or hiring manager has the time to review all the applicants. If the manager desires, they can also perform a text based (keyword) search to find resumes in the database of other candidates that may not have applied for the specific job but may qualify for the job. A keyword is a specific word or phrase the manager uses to find the most qualified candidates. Keywords are usually specific skills, tools, degrees, certifications, or acronyms. Due to a lack of time, resources, and other competing priorities, the individual must find ways to quickly filter out all applicants through a process of elimination or view only a subset of applicants. This exercise quickly becomes a process of Search Engine Optimization, commonly known as SEO. SEO is the process of optimizing content to rank highly in search results. The goal is to become the first result in a keyword search. In other words, the resumes most closely tailored to the keywords in a job description and requirements will be selected for review. For this reason, it likely and probable that a poorly targeted resume will never be viewed by a human being.

Another point to keep in mind is that most large companies have internal policies that require new job requisitions to be posted on the company website or externally via the internet for a period of one to two weeks. In some cases, you could call these jobs "zombie jobs", because they aren't really viable jobs as the hiring manager already has an internal candidate in mind. Some companies are gracious enough to provide this information in the job description, so don't waste your time on these listings.

To address the lack of internal HR resources for hiring, many large companies rely upon recruiting firms to farm their own databases and the Internet for the best, most qualified candidates. The process of using a variant of SEO still applies to this process. We shall discuss recruiting and contracting firms in the chapter covering the "Application Process".

Since the traditional large company job search process has deteriorated into an SEO exercise, there are several unfortunate outcomes from this trend:

1. Only candidates that performed the exact job at a prior employer and have a resume that closely matches the job description and requirements get noticed.

2. Candidates that performed a similar job with similar skills get missed since their resume was not tailored to the generic and/or industry specific job titles and descriptions.

3. Candidates, who in their prior roles were "generalists", fast learners, and "fast track" employees/managers, may be disadvantaged the most in a job search due to a lack of focus.

4. Corporations have become risk averse in taking a chance on hiring candidates that are not closely aligned to the job description, as there are literally hundreds of applicants that match the job description.

5. The old adage of "hire a good person that is trainable" is virtually lost. Companies hire entry level college graduates for entry level positions. For mid and later career candidates the chance to change careers without a significant drop in pay, responsibility, and title is hard to overcome.

6. Corporations rarely accept walk-in candidates, so the Internet has become a "wall" or barrier to overcome.

Your job search must be tailored to how the game is played or by using creative tactics. This workbook is focused on how the game is played, so don't be shy about coming up with creative ways to get your resume noticed.

Medium Sized Companies

With the advent of the internet and job boards, medium sized companies now act very similar to large corporations when hiring. Most of the techniques used to apply for a job at a large corporation apply equally to medium sized companies. However, medium sized companies may exhibit more flexibility in hiring candidates that aren't a perfect fit for a job description. These companies generally recognize that the "cream of the crop" candidates may already have work or job offers at large corporations, and they cannot always compete on equal footing with regards to salary and benefits. Job titles found online at industry comparison websites such as http://www.glassdoor.com may not reflect the salaries paid at medium sized companies. There can be large disparities between pay and benefits as compared to industry norms for a specific job. On the flip side, medium sized companies have been known to pay much higher salaries for key strategic employees that provide a competitive advantage to the company.

In terms of job search, medium sized companies may be more flexible and receptive to face to face job search strategies, so be creative!

Small Companies

The recommendations outlined in this workbook apply equally to small companies. The primary difference is that although you will be prepared to provide a world-class resume to these employers, you may find a range of professionalism when it comes to how they deal with candidates. Since small companies have few resources, they may or may not perform any number of tactics when hiring. These companies love to hire senior professionals with Fortune 500 company experience, as it provides them the knowledge to gain competitive advantage and continue to evolve the way they do business. They also have no problem hiring people with minimal education and experience since they know they can't always provide the salary and benefits typical of a large company. Small companies may also have unconventional policies when it comes to the interviewing process, dress, and grooming. An internet job search provides an efficient and cost effective tool for finding candidates, but these companies are even more inclined to hire someone they know based upon a personal reference and avoid the hassle of the hiring process all together. At the end of the day, if you follow the recommendations outlined in this workbook, you will be more than prepared to put your best foot forward at any small company.

Permanent Vs Contract Work

There was a time when most job listings were for permanent jobs. Permanent jobs are jobs that require the company to hire you as a permanent full or part-time employee. As an employee, there are many legal protections and perks extended to you. These include the right to certain benefits including health insurance and due process in regards to performance management and job separation. For the company, it includes a significant amount of paperwork and policies that must be followed. Oftentimes, a company hires a permanent employee only to find that they do not meet the job or behavioral requirements, which results in employee turnover.

Due to the high cost and risk of hiring new employees, many companies now use contracting to "test drive" an employee before making a formal permanent job offer. This is especially true in the Information Technology (IT) industry. As a contractor, the employee is technically an employee of the contracting company, typically a third party recruiting firm. The hiring company pays the recruiting firm an agreed contract hourly rate, and the recruiting firm pays the employee their agreed hourly salary and any benefits that have been negotiated or offered, which oftentimes includes health insurance. This relationship benefits all parties involved; the company pays a slightly higher hourly rate but saves on the high cost of hiring the wrong candidate. The recruiting company enjoys a profitable business model due to its inherent low overhead. The employee benefits by securing a job at a higher than customary hourly rate and the chance to prove themselves to be hired as a permanent employee. If you are out of work, do not be put off by contract work. You never know what door will open next.

The Role of Recruiting Firms

Recruiting firms play a necessary and important role in the modern hiring process. As mentioned earlier, they provide benefits to companies that use their services, and facilitate the match-making of employees to employers. Oftentimes, recruiting firms will pay recruiters a commission based upon placing an employee with a client (employer). Today, these recruiters may be the first people to view your resume and make a judgement call as to whether you have the skills to fill the role. Since they get paid when you are placed with an employer, they are your advocate.

At-Will Employment

Most U.S. public companies follow the doctrine of at-will employment. This allows either the employee or employer to terminate employment at any time for any cause without notice. While this concept remains controversial in some circles, the practical fact of the matter is that you are responsible for your own employability. If you do not maintain and/or update your job skills, or your behavioral skills are lacking, you put yourself at risk of being terminated. The day of getting a job early in your career and working that job until you retire is no longer reality. In the marketplace of ideas, you are required to be aware of the market and your role and value in it. It is necessary to take steps to ensure that your skills are the skills that employers need to produce the goods and services of the future. Ongoing career training or retraining for new skills is an investment in yourself and your own employability. When you find yourself out of work and needing to retool your skills, taking online courses or certifications can be a valuable asset in your job search. Better yet, if you are proactive and take these steps while you are employed, this can considerably reduce the time you spend between jobs.

Assumptions

There are several assumptions I make whenever I coach a job seeker. If you find yourself lacking in any of these areas, please don't be afraid to ask for help from a Trusted Advisor. Without meeting these pre-requisites, you are changing the dynamic from being ready and prepared to receive a job offer, to being lucky.

1. You have a strong desire to work hard, try your best, and be paid commensurate with your current market value.
2. You have abandoned the false belief that the world "owes" you something, like a good job, and you are humble enough to earn what you get through hard work and discipline.
3. You are motivated to aggressively pursue a new full time job by working full time to secure a new job.
4. You are confident enough in yourself to believe that you have value and a company would be fortunate to have you on their team.
5. You understand that getting a job is sales. You are selling yourself. You accept that even if you don't like sales that is what you *must* do. So put your best foot forward and *"go get the sale!"*
6. You recognize that in the market of talent many individuals will be "qualified" to secure a job offer, but the employer is looking for the "best fit". This may have nothing to do with how well you prepare, present yourself, or perform in an interview, and everything to do with the culture of the organization and/or team that is hiring.

7. You are free of all drugs. This includes marijuana.
8. You do not have a felony criminal record. A felony is a red flag to most employers so it makes securing a job much more difficult. Consider narrowing your job search to small companies or employers that actively hire candidates with felony convictions.

The Quick Win

You just lost your job and you are confident that with your large social and personal network you can quickly find a new job, possibly even a better one than your last. While many people find new jobs quickly based upon existing relationships, take a moment to consider the following before you send off your dusty resume to the world. My experience is that while a strong personal network is one of the most valuable tools to finding your next job, a resume that isn't optimized for the current job market and job listings may fall on deaf ears. Secondly, even if people know and like you, they probably have a pre-conceived notion of "what you do". Don't waste your most valuable resource with a resume that may not target the right opportunities.

For a quick win, first inform your network that you are looking for your next opportunity and wait to see what jobs are available. Once you have a job description and requirements, follow the steps in this workbook to customize your resume to that specific job and leverage your network to get it to the hiring manager. If followed correctly, you can bypass the Internet "wall", lead with your best resume for the job, and leverage your personal network to get a personal referral which, by the way, trumps almost anything any other candidate could offer. At the end of the day, a decision to hire is not based upon skills, it is based upon how the hiring manager feels about you as a candidate and how they feel you will fit into the job and the company culture.

Common Pitfalls

As you begin your career search you should be aware of several common pitfalls that can sidetrack and delay your path to success. As you follow the steps in this workbook to create and post your resume online, you will inevitably be contacted with offers for employment at several types of companies and industries that may look appealing, but are dead ends for most people. The insurance and financial services industries love to comb the internet for experienced job seekers that are looking for the freedom of running their own business or selling a product directly to consumers. The engagement typically starts with an email encouraging you to apply online. Once you apply online you are quickly swept into the hiring process and the euphoria of getting a professional job with unlimited salary potential. The sales pitch will make sense and seem achievable, but it will require some hard work and dedication on your part to bring it to fruition. Worst of all, it is one hundred percent commission, with no benefits, and you have to use your own vehicle to travel all over the state.

I have been lured into this business model more than once. Each time the pitch had enough upside for me to want to believe it would work. By taking this type of job there are several major drawbacks, though it may seem to be better than doing nothing at home. 1) You give up the eight to ten hours per day you should be using to find your next great job. 2) You expend your savings and scarce resources on a job that may pay, but not sufficiently well to support your family. In addition, since it is commission based, your pay is at risk every month due to unforeseen events, such as economic down-cycles. 3) You bear the burden of not having important benefits, such as health insurance.

Some opportunities, however, can be very rewarding. I have known individuals that learned what they could, and moved on to other full time jobs in the same industry. Conversely, there are many sales positions that are highly lucrative. The mortgage industry comes to mind, but during the Great Recession even that industry collapsed.

Many mid-career professionals seriously consider the option to start their own business and franchise. While these efforts can be financially rewarding, there are several pre-requisites that should be met before spending your 401k on your dream business. First, bear in mind that most franchises are basically a distribution model for a sound business. The best franchises are highly successful but typically require a large initial out-of-pocket investment on your part. Second, starting your own business requires that you put a business plan in place that helps ensure your success. Once you have a plan, getting a few key customers to build upon is key to ensuring the business' financial survival. Many entrepreneurs start big with facilities to support the eventual growth. Start small, and keep your costs as low as possible until you have the revenue to cover all your expenses. Third, don't confuse pyramid marketing schemes with a great business opportunity. A typical pyramid marketing scheme like Amway is basically a sales and distribution channel. Any company, whether good or bad, can adopt this go-to-market strategy, but most often we find companies with third tier products and poor financial backing pursue this avenue. This typically isn't the horse you want to tie your wagon to, especially with the downside risk of annoying all of your friends and family.

As a general rule of thumb, avoid commission only jobs that do not provide benefits. Companies that care about their employees typically provide a base salary with a commission incentive.

While we are on the subject of common pitfalls, let me state the obvious: securing a well-paying professional job *is* a full time job. Due to the pressures of life and financial obligations, many candidates take a low paying job to pay the bills only to find they don't have the time or energy to spend the required thirty to forty hours per week on their job search. The average professional job search will take three to six months of full-time work. My recommendation is that you sit down with your Trusted Advisor, make a budget, and decide how you will support yourself and family during unemployment. A short term sacrifice that gives you the time to get the right full-time job will pay dividends for years to come.

Planning

Moving on past the chance of a "quick win", let's focus on the most important part of your job search: putting a plan together for how you will target your efforts and optimize your resume. I know some of you are probably thinking, "I don't need a plan, I know what to do and I'm just going to go do it. I've got jobs before and I will do it again". This may be true, but your age, experience, job expectations, and the job market have all changed. By not creating a plan, you may be extending the time it takes to finally land that great job. If you are like most people, your goal is to get the best job you can as soon as possible. As Benjamin Franklin said, "If you fail to plan, you are planning to fail".

What I have found through my experience is that choosing to target your job search can be one of the hardest parts of finding a job. As we look across the thousands of jobs available online, it gives us a false sense of confidence that by not planning and targeting our job search we will still get something. How could we fail with so many opportunities?

This workbook was created in a step by step fashion to make it quick and easy to create your best resume. As the old adage goes, "How do you eat an elephant? Simple! One bite at a time." As part of the step by step process, tables have been included to help you write down and reference your own information at a later time when you start writing your resume. You can go back to any step, at any time, for a refresher of the material. Since the typical job applicant creates several resumes, you can follow the step by step approach for each new targeting strategy.

Good luck!

Step 1: Self-Assessment

The first step in planning is to perform an honest self-assessment. This includes mapping your formal and non-formal education as well as hard, behavioral, and transferrable skills. This self-assessment lays the foundation for the first third of your resume, and is critical to communicating what unique value you provide to an organization. If a human reads your resume, you have fifteen to twenty seconds to sell them on why you fit the job. A thorough self-assessment will help you craft the ideal elevator pitch about you.

FORMAL EDUCATION

Document your formal education. This includes any community college, four-year University, technical school, professional, online, vocational, accreditations, licenses, and certification work. If you completed coursework towards a degree or certificate, make sure you list the specific classes. When listing certificates, accreditations, licenses, or universities, make sure you include parenthesis () after the full name and include the abbreviation or acronym, if applicable. Do not use short-hand when documenting these accomplishments, as they will become the basis for your SEO optimized resume that needs to be keyword rich.

Table 1: Formal Education

School	Degree	City/State	Years Attended	Cumulative GPA	Awards & Recognitions
Acme State University (ASU)	Bachelors of Science in Computer Science (BSCS)	Acme, US	2010-2014	3.75	Honor Role

NON-FORMAL EDUCATION

Next, document your non-formal education. Non-formal education is a general term for education outside of a standard school setting. Though a degree may not have been earned, non-formal education can be highly enriching. For many jobs, non-formal education can be more valuable than formal schooling, so write down a few notes that may help when you draft your resume.

Table 2: Non-Formal Education

Education	Notes	Specials Tools & Skills	Years of Participation	Achievements
Auto Repair	Dad taught me how to rebuild a car	Welding, Soldering, Digital Multi-Meter (DMM), Calipers, Micrometer, Timing Gun	1998-2000	Restored a 1967 Chevrolet Camaro

Hard Skills

For the purpose of this workbook, a hard skill is a specific technical proficiency that has business value. For a software programmer hard skills may include a list of programming languages with which you have direct experience. Make sure when listing hard skills, you include any acronyms and ensure you use industry standard terms or lingo that you would expect to see in a job description or requirements.

Table 3: Hard Skills

Hard Skills	Certification/License	Achievements & Awards	Years of Experience
Journeyman Welder	Acme state welding license		2010-2014

Behavioral/Soft Skills

Behavioral or soft skills are traditionally not part of a formal education but are critical to your career success. These skills include interpersonal people skills, social skills, communication skills, character traits, attitudes, and your emotional intelligence. Employees that score high in these areas are typically recognized for their ability to work well with others. These people are often promoted into management positions and typically achieve greater success in the workplace than their peers. Generally, when an employee is fired, it is a result of poor behavioral skills, not a result of poor hard skills.

Companies typically use the annual performance appraisal and peer feedback to help employees improve their behavioral skills. If you have been challenged in these areas in the past, I suggest you read and implement the recommendations in Dale Carnegie's book "**HOW TO WIN FRIENDS AND INFLUENCE PEOPLE**".

Take a few minutes to write down some of your soft skills that co-workers, managers, friends, or family have complemented you on in the past. Understanding yourself and your own character traits will help you create an accurate summary of yourself for your resume.

Table 4: Behavioral Skills

Behavioral Skills	Awards & Recognitions
Peacemaker	Received the best team-member award at Acme Company

Transferrable Skills

Transferrable skills are the skills you acquire and demonstrate through your work that will go with you to your next job. These could include your ability to work quickly, problem-solve, and handle stress. Oftentimes, transferrable skills go un-considered when writing a resume, but will provide the key descriptors to characterize yourself when you fine tune your elevator pitch. For example, if you were an employer, would you rather read that John is an "experienced salesman" or would you rather read that John is an "experienced salesman that consistently crushes quotas"? Let me tell you, the *only* thing a sales manager is looking for is someone that can sell, not someone that is just experienced.

Table 5: Transferrable Skills

Transferrable Skill	Awards & Recognitions
Top Sales Producer	Received the Top Sales Producer award every year for the past 3 years

Trusted Advisor

In my experience one of the hardest parts of writing a great resume is condensing and summarizing what makes you unique and valuable in a simple two to three sentence elevator pitch. An elevator pitch is a short statement that you would use to tell someone on a short elevator ride why they should buy you, or hire you. To create the perfect elevator pitch, you need to know yourself and what type of person the hiring manager is looking to hire. While you will never know with certainty what the hiring manager is looking for, you can at least do your best in honestly describing yourself. One of the challenges of being human is that we all see ourselves differently than how we are perceived by others. For this reason, I highly recommend you spend some time with a *Trusted Advisor*. A Trusted Advisor is a person with whom you have come to know (preferably over time) and respect, has a good deal of education and work experience, and will honestly tell you about your best and worst qualities. A trusted advisor can be a friend, spouse, parent, co-worker, clergy, or prior manager. Don't be afraid to ask people for some advice in helping you create your best resume. Most people are happy to help a friend.

Step 2: Market Analysis

Step 2 includes understanding the overall economy and business climate, and where opportunities for your next job exist. For jobs that are highly specialized, this step may or may not apply, but for many job seekers, having an understanding of the broad, online, industry specific, or geographic markets, may yield some opportunities. As they say, "a high tide raises all ships", so if a specific industry or location has a high degree of hiring activity, it pays to know about it.

Broad Market

An excellent method for understanding the broad market is to create a daily routine of reading the business, finance, and economy sections of an online news aggregator. I personally use https://news.google.com/ each morning to keep me up to speed on what is happening nationally and around the world. A news aggregator scours the Internet for relevant news stories and post links to them in an easy to consume format. Skimming the headlines takes only a few minutes a day. As you create a habit of being informed about the economy and broad market, you will come to find new ways to target your job search. Almost every day there are new products being launched, new discoveries, or mergers and acquisitions. Each of these events can result in a company going on a hiring binge.

Online Job Market

When starting your online job search, it can be overwhelming when you see the number and diversity of online job posting services. Each online profile you create on a job board can take time, so it is more effective to target your search to a few key online websites and expand if the need arises at a later date. In the same way that Google News aggregates news stories from around the Internet, many online job boards aggregate job listings. Experienced job seekers tend to find that the same jobs are listed multiple times on each job board, by different recruiting firms, competing to fill the same job requisition. These same jobs are then posted on multiple job boards which results in a great deal of duplication. Add to that the fact that many online job listings are outdated, already filled, or following a company policy to post externally, and you end up with what at first looked like hundreds of opportunities ends up being only a handful. This can result in job seeker's becoming discouraged after applying for hundreds of jobs without any response. As a job seeker you need to prioritize the time you spend each day on the largest job aggregators, and focus on industry, trade, or skill-specific job boards.

For these reasons I recommend that job seekers looking for employment in the broad job market start by visiting http://www.indeed.com/. Indeed.com aggregates job listings from hundreds of job boards to create a master database. This gives you a good overall sense for what industries and companies are hiring, and paying, for certain positions. Indeed.com also offers an easy 1 click "apply" process, which significantly improves the speed at which you can apply for jobs. In addition, many job boards include the ability to create alerts. So when new jobs that match your alert are posted online, you are notified via email, text (SMS), or push notification. This can help ensure you don't miss the next opportunity.

Let's say for example that you were an oil industry training manager that was recently let go. You know from experience and reading the general news that the oil industry is in a multi-year slump. You review the online job boards by searching for "oil training manager" and you find virtually no jobs listed. This would be an indicator to you that creating a resume and applying for the few oil training manager positions has a very low probability of success. Assuming you have no other leads towards getting the same job, the lack of online job listings for this job should cause you concern. What you may notice however, is that there are a number of training manager positions posted for complimentary industries and companies. You may find that there is a plethora of Clean Energy Training Manager jobs. This would be a helpful data-point in determining which job title and/or industry on which you should focus.

Indeed.com does not aggregate job listings from many competing job boards such as Monster.com or industry specific job boards so this serves as only a broad market sample. Remember, a large percentage of jobs never get posted online so this is only a starting point for your planning activity.

Industry Specific Job Markets

In the previous oil industry example, the job seeker may have been misled from their research on Indeed.com because most of the oil industry jobs are listed on company specific websites and oil industry job boards such as http://www.rigzone.com. This pattern repeats itself for most large industries. To determine where you should be looking for industry specific job boards, just do a simple Google search for "[desired industry] job board". Once you know which job boards are the major sources of job listings, you can focus your daily search routine on those sites.

Geographic Job Markets

One of the great advantages of the Internet is that job seekers now have the visibility of employment postings around the world. When conducting your early planning analysis, you may find that by searching outside your local area, state, or even country, there are more opportunities than you were aware. Moving outside of your area comes with many sacrifices and added costs. Oftentimes, companies have a budget for relocation assistance or a hire-on bonus to compensate employees for what many recognize as a major sacrifice. On the flip side, looking elsewhere may give you the benefit of earning higher wages or benefits, especially if you currently live in a low cost area. There are many trade-offs to consider and higher wages do not always correlate to a higher standard of living. Wages typically lag housing costs, so buyer beware.

While the glamour and excitement of an international position may be enticing, there are many unseen costs which may include paying income taxes in both your home and working country. Most large companies offset these costs with expatriate benefits. Since international work is outside of the scope of this workbook, I highly recommend you research the full cost of international employment before accepting an offer.

Step 3: Career Selection

Career selection can be one of the hardest and most important aspects of your job search. Due to the nature of the internet and how resumes are stored, viewed, and filtered, finding a job requires that you focus your job search on a specific position that you know from your research is both in demand and correlates to your skills, experience, and education.

An example of a particular client's journey is instructive: Together, we spent three to four weeks trying to determine what the correct job title should be for him to pursue. He had spent many years in his industry and performed a multitude of different jobs. In his prior job, he had been highly valued, but his job title didn't reflect what the market was demanding, though he was technically over-qualified for many of the job opportunities. After many weeks of research, study, and consideration we finally settled on a title that would represent his skills and was in high demand. After two years of odd jobs and the all too common stint in retail, he landed a solid technical job within days of completing his resume.

The lesson to be learned is today's job market does not reward a generalist or "jack-of-all-trades". You must do your due diligence and force yourself to focus and narrow your job search. Choose what information to put forward for consideration in your resume. Your resume is not a legal document or an autobiography; it is your calling card or marketing brochure. In marketing, we know that you must tailor your message to your target audience. If you have information in your resume that doesn't support the story you are trying to tell for a specific job, remove it.

Where do I fit?

In this section I would like to give an example that hits close to home. If you are a mid-career professional, you may have had a number of job titles and experiences. For example, I have been a regulatory engineer, a technical marketing engineer, a sales engineer, and a product marketing engineer. These titles correlated well to the semiconductor industry, but did not correlate to other industries. In a traditional job search, a hiring manager may have viewed this steady progression of job and experience growth as a positive. But in the Internet Age this can actually be a weakness to a winning resume. My mistaken assumption was that any manager looking for an aggressive go-getter would hire and quickly train such a candidate, but since I did not tailor my resume to a specific job title that was in demand, my resume was mostly dismissed as not a good fit.

Candidates that take the time to analyze the market, assess their skills, and then present a resume that fits what the market wants, are much more likely to get an interview than those that cling to their own beliefs and assumptions that they are a great candidate with a strong historical resume. By recognizing this fact, we force ourselves to consider where we fit in the current job market. Once you make this informed decision, you can then optimize and target your resume to that specific job title, and to some degree, walk away from some of your prior job titles that you want to advertise on your resume.

Now when I say walk away from those prior job titles, I don't mean eliminate them from your resume completely. For example, if you were a marketing manager at your last job, it is likely that your responsibilities included much more than just marketing. You may have done sales, training, project management, customer service, or a number of other jobs. Now let's say that after doing your due diligence, you have decided that what the market wants isn't marketing managers, but sales managers. If you submit your marketing manager resume to the sales manager job listings, it is unlikely that you will be called for an interview because, as we mentioned earlier, the HR manager and recruiters are looking to fill a job requisition with the candidate that most closely matches the job description. This means you need to submit a sales manager resume.

In stating this recommendation, you may be thinking to yourself, "But I've never had the title of Sales Manager so I don't feel comfortable pitching myself in this way. Is this honest?" In targeting your resume I'm not suggesting that you mislead or make false statements. I'm suggesting that when you do your due diligence and consider what other jobs you may qualify for, there should be several natural and complementary job titles that make sense for your unique situation and experience. The example of a sales and marketing manager is an over-simplification of the analysis you and your Trusted Advisor should consider.

In some companies the difference between a sales and marketing manager is negligible, in other companies it is significant. Only you can determine if your experience can pass the "straight face test". This means if you were asked directly by an employer for examples of your experience as a sales manager, you could easily provide several examples from memory, without much trouble. If you can legitimately say you acted in the capacity of a sales manager in your prior job, then that is exactly what you should put on your sales manager resume.

Let me give you another example. The job title Product Marketing Engineer (PME) could translate across different industries and companies in the following ways: Product Marketing Manager, Product Engineer, Product Manager, Product Owner, Platform Owner, Enabling Engineer, Sales Engineer, Customer Engineer, Customer Support Engineer, Technical Marketing Engineer, and so on. Generally, Human Resource departments select generic job classifications and associated pay grades for simplification of record keeping and legal compliance. In this example a Product Marketing Engineer is the generic individual contributor job title for a technical employee in a specific industry. Many employees have this HR title, but their unique job description, if they have one, could span a wide number of work activities. By the way, once you take into account company size and industry, all the rules can change. For example, a PME at a Fortune 500 company may have similar responsibilities and job duties as a Vice President at a small company. In the financial services industry, the title of Vice President is carried by almost everyone, even many recent college graduates. This is because of the industry specific dynamics of titles and what they convey to a target audience or customer. Titles do not always correlate well across company sizes and industries, so don't assume that your last job title is the only one you can use to create your resume or marketing brochure.

Online Analysis

A thorough online job market analysis is probably the quickest and easiest path to narrowing down your target job title. As mentioned earlier, reviewing the broad job market on job boards such as Indeed.com or visiting industry and skill specific job boards is a great way to get a feel for what positions are available. Many individuals approach their job search from the perspective of wanting to do something completely new. Unfortunately, in the Internet Age, a strong targeted resume with increasing experience in the same field, industry, or expertise is typically rewarded with interviews, versus candidates that are trying to re-invent themselves. If you are committed to completely changing your career direction, I recommend that you pursue ongoing education for your new career field and engage career counselors that have expertise in that field. Unfortunately, this path typically takes much more time than most candidates can afford. For mid-career professionals it is often easiest to continue their job search in a related field, discipline, or industry. These resumes will be the most targeted and successful at securing an interview.

As part of your online analysis, you should become well versed in what your target job requirements are and your own level of seniority to fill a position. Individuals sometimes seek positions that include a promotion, in hopes of making a positive step onward and upward through their job search. My experience has proven that this strategy is flawed. Most employers are typically looking for candidates that have several years of experience in a specific job title before they take the risk of hiring someone they have only interviewed. This goes back to the adage of behavioral interviewing which we shall review later. The premise is that a candidates' prior experience is the best indicator of future success. If you were previously a manager, it is unlikely a new employer would hire you as a director. On the other hand, if you are currently employed and a company is looking to promote you away from your existing employer, this strategy works well and benefits both parties. Don't expect to get the promotion if you are currently out of work.

Table 6: Target Job Titles

Job Title	Job Title
Marketing Manager	Sales Manager

Salary Analysis

The goal of having gainful employment is to be able to provide for our families and financial obligations. Therefore, It is not unusual for job seekers to use their job search as an opportunity to increase their financial position in life, and benefit with a higher salary. While job seekers earn higher salaries every day, you must be careful not to torpedo your employment search with unrealistic salary expectations. I recommend that you spend some time researching your target job title on websites like http://www.salary.com to get a good feel for what type of salary you can expect. In addition, it is typical practice for recruiters to cold call candidates and immediately ask, "What is your hourly rate?" Having done your research will give you the information to easily respond to these queries with minimal effort. The standard number of hours in a US work year is 2,080, for your hourly rate calculations. Just take the hourly rate and multiply it by 2,080 to find the target annual salary. For example, if you earn $10 per hour, your annual salary would be $20,800.

Keep in mind that salaries can vary based upon geographic location, market climate, and experience. Job seekers tend to look at the higher range of salaries and thus tend to feel that they deserve the highest possible wage within the pay range. These pay ranges are typically very broad to accommodate a myriad of candidate experience levels, so tread carefully when communicating salary expectations.

In an interview scenario, it is oftentimes a safer strategy to employ the Socratic Method by answering a question with another question. If an interviewer, not a recruiter, asks what your salary requirements are, it is better to ask what the published pay range is for the position or ask, "What is the typical salary for someone with my experience and education?" Once again, don't torpedo yourself by leading with a high number. This may automatically disqualify you from consideration.

A friend of mine once said, "For important decisions, it is best to wait until the last possible moment to make the decision. That is when you will have the most information to make the best choice". The salary question is critical, so don't rush into it.

Industry analysis

A key part of your planning activity is to understand the industry, or industries, which you will be targeting. Oftentimes, a candidate has a good understanding of their most recent employer, but that doesn't provide a full picture from which to target their job search. An invaluable research tool in this activity is http://www.google.com/finance. At Google Finance and other similar websites, you can start to map all the various possibilities and paths for you to pursue which are directly and indirectly involved in your target industries. As I mentioned earlier, you will have a much higher chance of securing a job within an industry in which you have experience versus one that you do not. Some industries, in fact, appear to be completely closed to candidates that don't have direct experience, such as the medical industry.

Finance websites, like Google Finance, are geared towards business news, stock, and company information. If you have spent any time around public company stock market disclosures, you will already know that companies tend to communicate about the health of their business through securities filings. These websites are a great source to learn about your target industry, major competitors, suppliers, and customers. This information will become the cornerstone to your job search.

The following graphic shows the typical information for a large company like General Electric (GE) on Google Finance:

Figure 1: Industry Analysis

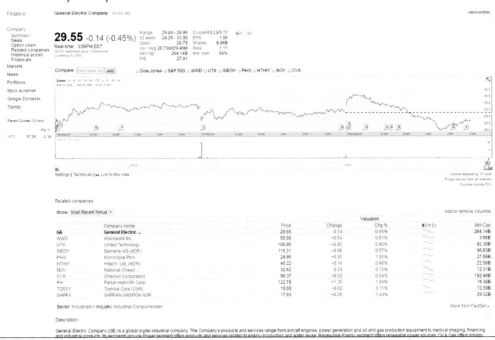

As you can see from the graphic, it lists the company's stock information. This can provide valuable insight into the company's financial health. Below the stock market chart are related companies. These are companies in the same or similar industries that you can add to your target search list. As you read further, you will find key suppliers and customers that can also be valuable targets for a job search. The thinking goes like this: If you are an expert on the Acme Product Machine, it is very likely that Acme's competitors, suppliers, and customers would be more likely to hire you than any other random applicant.

In the table below list the following information from your industry and company research:

Table 7: Target Industries, Competitors, Suppliers & Customers

Target Industry	Major Competitors	Suppliers	Major Customers
1. Manufacturing	ACME Products Inc.	123 Widgets Inc.	Warner Brothers Productions
2.			
3.			
4.			
5.			
6.			
7.			
8.			
9.			
10.			

Execution

Step 4: Creating Your Resume

Now that the planning phase is complete, you should have an idea of a few job titles and industries that you will target for your search. You should feel comfortable with the following points before creating your resume:

- You are a good fit and qualified for the job title (this includes skills, experience and education). If you apply to jobs for which you are underqualified in terms of prior experience or education, you are wasting your time.
- You have found and selected a well-written job description from an online job listing that you will use to customize and target your resume. (This is like taking a test with the answers in your hand.)
- You have completed the self-assessment and tables one through seven in the prior chapters of this workbook.
- You have the right behavioral skills to secure a job offer and work well with co-workers, once you start the job.
- You understand and accept the average salary for the job title in the geographic markets in which you will be applying for work.

If you can answer yes to all of the above questions, you are ready to customize and target your resume for success.

Purpose

The purpose of a resume is not to summarize all of your work history. It is a calling card and an advertisement to employers that you have the skills, experience, and education to fulfill the duties of the job listed. Most of us fall into the trap of thinking our resume is a historical document for us to look back on with fondness. There is certainly a need for all of us to have a long form historical resume, but this is not what we use to get employers attention in a crowded market of thousands of job listings and millions of applicants. Your goal is to stand out and advertise yourself as the perfect fit for a specific job. This means that your resume must be hyper-targeted to a specific job. If you want to target multiple jobs, you will need to create several resumes that target each specific job. This is completely normal and gives you a better chance at finding something.

Plan to create your first resume for the job you feel you are most qualified to fill. Many people think they can use this chance to move up the career ladder to a higher job title than they had previously. Employers may hire you into a higher job title, but it is more likely for them to hire candidates in the same title as they had previously. If you want a promotion, work hard to get it after you are hired, not during the hiring process. Misguided expectations that do not match the expectations of a potential employer can result in prolonging the time to a job offer.

Scope

The scope of your resume should cover your most recent work experience that applies to the target job, your education, and applicable skills. In addition to these basic requirements, a resume should articulate why the hiring manager should interview you over all the other candidates. To a hiring manager or recruiter, most of the resumes look very similar, with all the same skills and acronyms that match the job description. The resume elevator pitch and highlighted accomplishments sections are your chance to stand out and state your case, so embrace this chance and don't be afraid to brag a little!

When creating your resume, there is a tendency to list everything that you have accomplished. With your Trusted Advisor, use good judgement to only include information that is relevant to the job requirements and supports the story you are trying to tell about you. The goal is to create a simple and clean one-page resume, two pages maximum. Occasionally employers will ask if you have a longer form resume, which you can have ready as a backup. For candidates with a long work history, I recommend that you remove some of the oldest jobs on your resume, unless you feel they are critical to telling your story. Employers typically care most about what you have done in the last 5-15 years, so save the older work history for your long form resume.

Structure

Figure 2 provides an example of what I recommend as the structure and required information for a single page resume. This template is also available at: http://www.howtogetanonlinejob.com. In the following section we will review each piece of the resume and how to present your story in a way that consistently gets you noticed.

Figure 2: Resume Template

YOUR NAME HERE

Address, City, State Zip ◆ Phone ◆ your.email@gmail.com

JOB TITLE (SPECIFIC TITLE IN THE JOB DESCRIPTION)

Keywords / Tags / Skills / Certifications / Software Languages / Industries

Use this short paragraph as your elevator pitch. Imagine if you had only 30 seconds to tell the hiring manager why they should hire you...no frills, just straight talk. "This is why I'm so awesome". If this sentence or two doesn't jump right off your lips when you say it out loud, rewrite it. Make sure this briefly summarizes why they should hire you and the qualities (adjectives) that you possess that align to the behavioral skills that make you the perfect fit for the job.

HIGHLIGHTED ACCOMPLISHMENTS

This is where you substantiate your elevator pitch with two to three of your best accomplishments that set you apart from other candidates. Provide a 1-2 sentence explanation. Include the measurable impact. Use metrics such as revenue generated, cost saved, or new enrollments to highlight how your efforts contributed to the bottom line. Example: As the East Coast sales manager I personally identified and closed 50 new sales that resulted in $2M of incremental revenue to Acme Corporation.

Provide a 1-2 sentence explanation. What was the measurable impact?

Provide a 1-2 sentence explanation. What was the measurable impact?

EDUCATION

This section should meet the major education requirements that are listed in the target job description. List the highest degree first, your GPA (if it >3.5) and any honors you received. If you don't have any college degrees, licenses or certifications omit this section. If you are currently enrolled in a degree program move this paragraph to the end of the resume and list your expected graduation date.

Bachelors of Science in Business Administration (BSBA), Acme University, City, State, 2012 (optional), Valedictorian GPA: 4.0

Certification, School, Year Received (optional)

CAREER HISTORY

Job Title, Company name Year - Present. 2-3 sentences describing the job scope and key accomplishments.

Job Title, Company name Year - Year. 2-3 sentences describing the job scope and key accomplishments.

Job Title, Company name Year - Year. 2-3 sentences describing the job scope and key accomplishments.

Leisure: I enjoy xyz (optional).

NAME

In the name section, list at least your first and last name. This is a marketing document so be professional, but if there is a nickname you think will not detract from the presentation feel free to use it.

CONTACT INFORMATION

List your basic contact information. Many online jobs boards automatically extract this information and pre-populate your online profile, so feel free to list your address, phone, and email. Make sure the email you provide is your personal email address and not a work email address. You want to keep all your personal correspondence separate from work correspondence for many reasons. If you don't have a personal email address you can register for one online from many Internet providers or companies, such as Google, that offer Gmail as a free service (go to http://www.Gmail.com and register for an account).

When submitting your resume to recruiters, you may find that your contact information has been removed from the version the employer receives. This is a customary business practice as the recruiter wants to maintain control of you as a candidate and prevent employers from doing an end-run-around.

JOB TITLE

The job title of your resume should *exactly* match the job title for which you are applying. You have about twenty seconds of an employer's time. If the job title does not match, it will immediately send a message that you are not the "perfect fit" and you risk being discarded before the employer even reads your elevator pitch.

KEYWORDS

The keyword section of your resume is new to many candidates and may seem to clutter the view, but it plays several important roles.

Firstly, the keyword section quickly shows the hiring manager that you have a few key skills that he/she needs to fill the role. With only fifteen to twenty seconds to view a resume, this could be the ticket to getting on a short list of candidates.

Secondly, going through the exercise of reviewing the keywords in your target job description and listing out all the skills and acronyms that describe you, will help you recall important skills and acronyms you may have overlooked when drafting your resume.

Third, the keywords are the foundation of your SEO strategy. Most simple databases use a keyword search to filter and locate candidates. Recruiters or HR managers may not understand the specifics of the job they are trying to fill, but they will know what keywords to use to find the best candidates online or via their HR database.

Assuming that all resumes have the same keywords, how does the database determine which resumes to show in the database search results and in what order? While advanced search engines like Google use advanced algorithms to find the best contextual fit, most job database search engines use basic keyword searches and prioritize according to the existence and frequency of the keyword or phrase. If the recruiter is looking for a Java developer, how many times do you think you should list Java as a keyword on your resume? Use keywords and key-phrases generously but without detracting from the overall quality and presentation of the resume.

The keyword section gives you another chance to list out and repeat the keywords or phrases you expect a recruiter or hiring manager would use to find candidates. We know from Internet search engine analytics that over ninety percent of consumers click on the first few links on the first page of search results. If you are on the second page, good luck. The same premise holds true for resume SEO.

List the keywords or phrases that occur in your sample target job description you found online (when choosing a sample job description make sure it is well written and keyword rich).

Table 8: SEO Keywords and Phrases

Keyword/Phrase	Acronym	Keyword/Phrase	Acronym
Project Management Professional Certification	PMP Certification	Certified Financial Planner	CFP

ELEVATOR PITCH

An elevator pitch is what you would say to the hiring manager if you had the good fortune to ride up a few floors on an elevator, and you knew this was your last chance to have him consider you as a candidate. Your desperate, you've done all your due diligence, you know the type of person he wants and that you're the perfect fit! What do you say? Well, whatever it is, make sure its short, direct, and to the point.

I like to put myself into the hiring manager's shoes when creating this section for a candidate. I typically ask the question, "what qualities make a good candidate for this job?" An example would be "what qualities make a great salesperson?" From experience, I can tell you a few qualities that make a great salesperson. These would be: 1. A hard worker. 2. Someone that enjoys people. 3. Competitive people, such as athletes. With this short list I can start to map my qualities from Table 4 and match them up to the qualities that make a naturally gifted salesperson.

In Table 9, list the qualities that you feel make a naturally gifted employee for your target job title, and then match this list up to your own qualities from Tables 2-5. Use this as a reference tool when writing your elevator pitch, meaning don't use these words specifically, but use them as guides to help you think how you should present yourself in the elevator pitch.

Table 9: Gifted Qualities

Gifted Qualities for Target Job	Gifted Qualities for Target Job
Social Butterfly	Competitive

HIGHLIGHTED ACCOMPLISHMENTS

The highlighted accomplishments section is your chance to substantiate your elevator pitch of why you are great with a few quantifiable examples. Make sure your examples apply to the specific job at hand. Listing accomplishments that don't support the story you are trying to tell may confuse or distract the employer.

I find coming up with a short list of accomplishments isn't that hard, however, the hardest part is making them measurable. If, for example, you helped a customer start a production line because your equipment was down and needed repairing, it may be hard to estimate the impact. Just come up with what you feel is a reasonable estimate that would pass the straight face test in an interview. Most run rates for manufacturing lines are well understood. If it was an average bottling plant, you may be able to do an Internet search and find the average daily production for a bottling plant is 100,000 bottles. With your industry experience, you can estimate what the value or revenue impact would be if the production facility wasn't producing, Spend some time to think about your accomplishments that most directly relate to the job at hand, and use real or estimated numbers to communicate the business impact. At the end of the day, employers want to know exactly *how* you will help them to design, develop, or deliver their product or service.

EDUCATION

The education section is most likely the last section a recruiter or manager will review to determine if your resume deserves a thorough read or not. You will have to decide whether your education should be highlighted or moved near the bottom of your resume based upon your situation.

If you have a solid educational foundation, it is important to put this out there. I once worked with a client that had graduated from one of the top universities in the country for his discipline but failed to point it out in his resume. You worked hard to get that education, so don't be afraid to lead with a compelling degree and any highlights that showcase your education or honors.

For new college graduates, your education and GPA may be the primary determining factor as to whether you get an interview or not. When I worked at Intel, I found that most candidates wouldn't be considered unless their GPA met a certain number. Make sure you highlight your high GPA if it is over 3.5, but don't lead with GPA if it is low.

Another area of educational achievement that often goes overlooked, is the honors you received while at school. If you were on the Honor Roll or were a Valedictorian or another designation of honor, make sure to include it.

For candidates that do not have a strong educational story, you may want to emphasize licenses or certifications that apply to the target job. If you have little or no education, you don't want to advertise that fact, so move any education you have to the bottom of your resume and let your experience and accomplishments tell the story of why you're a great candidate.

Many candidates have education that applies to the job title but they may not have finished a degree due to any number of reasons. An example would be a client who finished all but two classes to complete a degree but did not graduate due to being relocated out of state. In this situation, it made sense to list all the major classes he had completed and the reason for not completing the degree.

A final thought that also supports your resume SEO strategy is to list degrees that are in progress. If a certain job has a requirement for a BSBA degree, which you don't currently have, you could also state that you are currently completing your coursework towards a BSBA degree with an estimated graduation date. That way, you get the SEO benefit of having the degree even though you may not have been awarded it yet. The same SEO strategy works for professional licenses and certifications. If a job requires a certification, go ahead and start down the path of getting the certification and list it as 'in progress' on your resume.

CAREER HISTORY

The career history section is important to not only communicate your past experience, but to show how said experience makes you the ideal candidate. If you have had many job titles and responsibilities, it may or may not tell a logical story for how your career has evolved to make you the best fit for the job. Employers don't want to be confused by a career history that jumps around different jobs, industries, has unexplained gaps, steps backward, or is hard to explain. You should keep your own history of actual job titles and dates etc. for reference, but don't clutter your resume with this information.

Approach your career history as you would tell a story that makes logical sense. Do not state things that may create red flags, prompt probing questions, or put you out of consideration. A common scenario is when mid-career professionals struggle to find their next job and take a low paying job in the interim. Conversely, having a large span of time, without being employed, is also considered a negative, so carefully consider how you will list your career with your Trusted Advisor in a way that is accurate but doesn't disadvantage you.

Say for example, you were a professional manager for 10 years, then after a layoff, you ended up taking a job in retail to pay your bills. If you lead with the retail job as your last position, this will automatically create a flag and question in the employer's mind. Do not lead with these kind of jobs on your resume, unless that is your career path and it fits the target job. Take some time to consider what other work or business opportunities could fill the space of time, if it was more than a few months. Many mid-career professionals take side consulting jobs or start their own business during unemployment. If this is the case, this shows you have the skills and aptitude to fill your time with other productive ventures, as opposed to working in a retail store which could signal any number of potential employability issues. If the employer or recruiter thinks you have employability issues, they will spend twenty seconds on your resume and then move on to the next candidate.

As discussed previously, many job titles have responsibilities that could fit any number of job requirements. You should take the time to select the right prior job title and job description that makes truthful and logical sense for the job that you are targeting. For example, if you were a marketing manager that performed sales duties, you may change the prior job title to Salesperson and describe what sales job duties you performed. A typical client of mine will list their last job as the actual title of marketing manager, list the marketing job duties they fulfilled, then turn around and apply for a sales position. This makes no sense at all. Employers and recruiters are only looking for candidates that have prior sales experience and say so on their resume.

This same approach to communicating your job title and responsibilities should be continued through the Career History section of your resume. If you reach a point, several jobs down the page, where your experience no longer relates to your target job title, then that would be the logical place to stop listing your experience. However, if you believe the prior work history would clearly differentiate you for the job, or supports the story you are trying to tell, then list it. Again, there are no set rules in marketing, you just need to put your best foot forward and tell a story that makes sense.

One aspect of Career History that some candidates struggle with is how much detail to provide about their prior jobs. For example, if you worked at a company for 10 years and had 3 different job titles, do you list each job and responsibilities, or just the most recent? I would like to think that most employers value seeing the detailed progress of your career if it tells a story of continual growth, education, and greater responsibility. If this is the case, list all the jobs at that company. If you need to save room and it makes minimal difference to your target job, condense them into one job title and description. Make sure your summary description is brief and relates to your target job title.

So, what should you include in the Career History section? If you are working hard to present a concise one-page resume (which I highly recommend for the first contact), I like to list the company, dates of employment, job title, and a short description of your responsibilities. Your accomplishments should have already been captured in the Highlighted Accomplishments section of your resume, so you don't need to beat the drum too much more if they were impactful.

If you are creating your long form resume, I like to include the company, dates of employment, job title, a short description that explains the company and industry, and your measurable accomplishments and responsibilities. Again, tie any accomplishments to measurable metrics that you can repeat in an interview when asked.

When listing dates of employment, I prefer to list only the year to year range. I typically avoid getting into the details of days or months on a resume. Some employers, especially those in government or financial services, may require you to provide a complete history of employment without any time gaps. This is good information to have in a reference document, but don't clutter your resume with it. If you do, it typically shows unwanted gaps in employment that could be a potential red flag or prompt the interviewer to ask questions that you would rather avoid. The resume is a marketing brochure, so always put your best foot forward.

LEISURE
I like to include a Leisure section at the bottom of the resume, just to give the employer some insight into the type of person I am outside of work. Highlight activities that are a net positive and cannot be interpreted as negative. I usually list my hobbies that includes exercise and sports. Individuals that exercise typically work hard to stay healthy and this gives the impression that you will also work hard and take fewer sick days. For some jobs, extracurricular activities are the key flag to an employer that you are the type of candidate they are looking for.

If you participate in charitable organizations, this can often be interpreted as a positive since it shows you care for others and give back to the community. Corporate responsibility is a popular topic today, so for companies that make a point of serving in the community, this could make the difference to getting an interview or not. For companies that do not actively pursue social agendas, this will have only a neutral impact.

If you participate in religious or political organizations, this could be positive or negative. For this reason, I recommend that you do not list your religious or political affiliations. Your resume is a marketing brochure, so don't prejudice an employer against you before they have even met you. If, however, your target job directly involves religious and political organizations, then by all means, share your experience in these areas.

WRITING STYLE

A poorly written resume is the fastest and easiest way to get disqualified from consideration. Of all the resumes I have reviewed, I can personally tell you that if a resume is wordy, poorly written, or has spelling errors, I see no reason to contact that candidate. My feeling is that if the candidate cannot present themselves well on their own marketing brochure (i.e. resume), how on earth are they going to impress me at work? When employers screen resumes they are looking for any reason to weed you out from the pile. Don't give them that chance!

The writing style for your resume should be business and professional. This means to the point and free of all grammatical and spelling errors. If, however, your target job is in a creative discipline, such as graphic arts, all bets are off. In that scenario I would encourage out of the box thinking and creativity when presenting your resume. Do it in a way that you feel highlights your talents and sets you apart from the pack. Just keep in mind that when your resume is uploaded to a company's hiring database, most graphics and formatting will be lost and this could potentially back-fire on you. To mitigate this risk, you might consider a standard text resume for uploading and then a more creative version for interviews.

The resume format and layout can become a critical factor if your resume looks woefully deficient compared to others. While it is true that many resumes are uploaded into databases that strip the formatting away, you will still need to have a presentable version for interviews. I find that even for phone interviews sharing a nicely formatted resume can help the interviewer and set you apart from the crowd. A resume template that will avoid any layout deficiency issues is available for download at http://www.HowToGetAnOnlineJob.com.

I have found that most professionals benefit from having a Trusted Advisor or third party review their resume before publishing. Candidates tend to put massive amounts of time into their resume and oftentimes miss obvious things just because they have worked on it for so long. Remember to be as concise as possible. Oftentimes saying each sentence out loud will give you the necessary feedback to know if a change is needed. If you know that you are not a strong writer, get some help.

PAPER

While much of the job search process occurs online, there is still a place for a well-presented resume during the interview. Oftentimes the hiring manager will come to the interview with a piece of paper that loosely resembles the beautiful resume you originally submitted to the employer. HR databases tend to strip away all the formatting and leave you with a poorly structured document that is hard to read and follow. Why not take this opportunity to put a beautiful resume in each of the interviewer's hands? Bring enough copies for as many managers as you think will interview you. The face to face interview is your chance to put forth the real you. If you start the interview by presenting each interviewer with a nicely printed and formatted resume on heavy resume paper, it starts the discussion off on the right foot. Remember, you are selling yourself! Don't ever use cheap printer paper.

Step 5: Your Online Brand

Now that you have put a plan in place, selected a target job title, and created a beautiful resume, you are ready to optimize your online brand. The Internet has provided employers with yet another easy tool to screen candidates before they take another step in the hiring process. Many Millennials and Gen X'er's have spent copious hours reading and posting articles on social media websites and apps without the slightest thought to how this might impact their employment. It is now generally accepted that some colleges review a potential student's online postings before extending acceptance to attend the school. In a similar fashion, progressive employers review a candidate's online profile to learn as much as they can before taking the next step in the hiring process. For these reasons, it is important that you make sure your online brand reflects the story your resume tells, and the type of person you think an employer is looking to hire. Your online presence isn't limited to just the comments and/or articles that you have authored. Employers can get a broader picture of you as an individual by reading about your views, likes, dislikes, and personality from multiple online sources. This also includes which feeds you subscribe to and which articles you repost or comment on via your social media profile.

Some of you may be thinking, "well, I don't have to worry about my online brand because I *have* no online brand". That may be true, but for candidates looking to work in the modern economy not having a professional LinkedIn profile could signal to an employer that you are behind the times, and most likely not a good fit for the job. For this reason, I recommend that you seriously consider your online brand and take steps to align it with your career goals.

LINKEDIN

Of all the social websites I have used, LinkedIn provides a great service and personal value. For those of you unfamiliar, LinkedIn is essentially Facebook for professionals. The focus is on connecting professionals to each other and helping build careers. It also includes job search capabilities. As your career evolves, you will come in contact with thousands of people. These relationships tend to fade over time and career changes. LinkedIn gives you the ability to stay in contact with coworkers and create an online resume or profile. It also allows you to ask for recommendations from prior managers, mentors, or peers, and get to a decision maker when applying for work.

The value of a strong professional network cannot be understated. As your career evolves, you will come across many people that have the personality along with the skills and/or experience that you value. From a purely social perspective, I have found joy in being able to stay in contact with friends that are separated by many years of work and geographical distance.

The relationships you establish at work are often the most powerful and effective tools in your job search. Over time, your network will spread across many companies and these friends are uniquely positioned to help you in your time of need. First, you can use sites like LinkedIn to find who in your network is hiring. Second, you can leverage your personal relationships to bypass the Internet wall and find a direct connection to the hiring manager. And third, these individuals have already worked with you so they can provide an honest and unvarnished assessment of your work ethnic which can oftentimes result in a quick interview and offer.

When you create a LinkedIn account, it gives you the opportunity to document your professional profile. I recommend that you take your target job resume and cut and paste most of the content into your LinkedIn profile. When your profile is coupled with endorsements and recommendations from past co-workers, managers, and peers, it becomes a powerful tool to characterize and validate who you are as an individual. Since most hiring decisions come down to a gut feeling as to which candidate would be the best fit for the job, a complete LinkedIn profile removes much of the risk in a hiring decision.

If you don't have any recommendations on LinkedIn yet, create your profile, make sure it is complete, then navigate to the "Ask for Recommendations" section as shown in Figure 3. The idea behind Ask for Recommendations is that you can request direct online recommendations from senior managers or anyone that you have worked with in the past. These recommendations can then be posted with your approval to your LinkedIn profile page. Obviously, ask those people that would leave a positive review of your capabilities. Senior manager recommendations carry more weight than co-worker recommendations. You could also request recommendations from professors, deans, or instructors from a certification or licensing program.

Figure 3: LinkedIn Recommendations

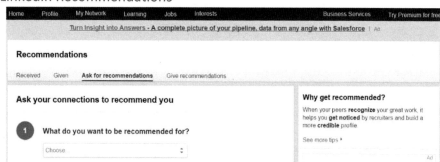

INTERNET CLEAN-UP

Now that you have created your own Internet brand, you need to make sure there aren't any skeletons left around the Internet that could damage your chance of getting a job offer. Online job sites are replete with stories of employers not hiring candidates due to information they found online. Now is the time to make sure that your private life is private and that nothing online could come back to bite you.

As a general rule, the information you author or post online should be positive and reflect well on you as a person. If you post information online related to your field of work, it reinforces your story of being a qualified candidate that loves their work. Any negative information about you will be interpreted as such by a potential employer. This could include Tweets, authored content, photos, or videos of your personal life, and yes that includes your college life. Content that shows or implies that you have used marijuana or illegal drugs or exercised poor judgement would be an immediate red flag.

The first step is to perform a simple Google Search on your name at http://www.Google.com and review any information that is publicly available about you. If you have Tweets, pictures, videos, or articles that could be construed in a negative light, take steps to remove them. Even if photos or videos are not controversial, it's a good idea to make sure they are tasteful and show you in a positive light.

Finally, if you want to keep your social life totally private, visit social media sites such as Facebook and update your privacy and security settings to only share your information with those you allow.

Step 6: How To Approach The Application Process

The following steps are ordered by priority to help you get the most benefit from your job search in the shortest possible time. For each target job title and resume you create, repeat this process.

1. Leverage Your Personal Network

   It goes almost without saying that your personal network of family, friends, relatives, and co-workers will be your best and most effective tool to finding your next job. Before emailing your resume to everyone, test the waters by letting your network know that you are in the job market. That way, if a lead is provided, you still have the chance to customize your resume for the job opportunity. Be careful of how you communicate. If you use an online social tool, consider the implications of creating a public record of your job search. Employers may find your announcement months later and it may tell a different story than your resume. Face to face contact is the preferred method when dealing with your personal network.

2. Job and Career Fairs

   If you are a recent college graduate or a mid-career professional, job and career fairs are excellent places to meet face to face with employers and break through the

Internet wall. Make sure to prepare your best resume and print out multiple copies on quality paper in preparation for the event. Wear your best clothes to make an impactful first impression. Consider a pressed suit or dry cleaned modest dress.

3. Engage Recruiting Firms

As part of creating a job search strategy, identify at least 3 recruiting firms that serve your targeted industry. This can be accomplished in a matter of minutes by doing a Google search. For example:

- Type "https://www.Google.com/" into your web browser on any computing device.
- Search for specific recruiters in your area and field. For example, "IT recruiting firms in Atlanta".
- View the search results in sponsored and "organic" ads (i.e. not paid ads) for Atlanta IT recruiting firms.
- Spend some time to create a list of the top firms and then submit your resume online to their website. This puts you in their database for current and future reference.
- Once you have submitted your resume, follow up with a phone call and try to set-up a face to face introduction so they can get to know you.

Once the recruiter has personally met you, they are more likely to forward your resume to one of their clients when a new job requisition is posted, which is typically every week. A good relationship with a recruiter means more job opportunities for you.

4. Target Specific Companies, Suppliers and Customers in Your Industry

The skills and experience from prior jobs are valuable, and companies often hire employees from within the same industry. Even if you have the qualifications to perform a job, if you don't have direct industry experience, it may put you out of consideration. For this reason, you should target companies in the same industry with which you have spent most of your career. Use the list of companies you created in Table 7 and create profiles on each company's website. Even if the company isn't hiring at the current time, they will keep your resume for at least six to twelve months in case they have a hiring need. Once you have created your profile, search for available jobs and apply for those that match your target job title. This process may also open your mind to other similar jobs that are available. Write down these other job titles for later reference in case you want to target them at another time. In addition, some company's websites allow you to create alerts for when specific job openings occur. Sign up for these alerts so you can respond as soon as jobs are posted online. Many company policies require that jobs are posted online for at least one week. By setting up alerts, you reduce the odds that you will miss a great opportunity.

Just as working in the same industry is critical to your work experience, many of your industry's suppliers value your experience. Oftentimes, experience can only be gained at work, so applying to your industry's supplier base can also put you on a short list of qualified and experienced candidates. Use the suppliers list in Table 6 to create a profile, and apply for work on each suppliers' company website. Write down any other complementary job titles you find for future reference. Sign up for job alerts.

Use the Customer list you created in Table 7 and follow the same process as above to target each of your industry's largest customers. Write down any other complementary job titles you find for future reference and sign up for those job alerts as well.

5. Create Online Profiles On Job Boards

With the plethora of online job boards, it can be confusing to know where to present yourself and where to spend your time. To cover the basics, I recommend you post your resume on at least one broad market, one industry specific, and one skill-specific job board. This strategy will cover 40-60% of the online job postings in your market and help you avoid some common pitfalls of posting on the wrong sites. There's nothing wrong with posting to multiple sites, but sometimes candidates can spend countless hours posting and applying for jobs without any response because of posting to the wrong site. By following the 80/20 rule, you can target specific job boards and get the most bang for your buck.

In terms of broad market job boards, I would recommend two which are always at the top of my list. I like Indeed.com because, as a job board aggregator, it includes many job listings from all types of job boards across the Internet. Indeed.com is a good sampling of broad market jobs, but many private companies aren't included in their listings, so I also recommend Monster.com. Monster.com has the brand presence to cover a large percentage of hiring companies. Create a profile, create target job alerts, and then go ahead and apply for your target job listings. Don't be discouraged if responses are slim the first few weeks as most Internet job postings are probably already several weeks old. It will take a few weeks of concerted effort before you to start applying to new job postings. Job posting alerts will help you in your daily job search by giving you a short list of new jobs for which to apply. If you have a smartphone, download the Indeed and Monster smartphone apps from the iTunes or Android App Stores. These applications also have an easy "one-click to apply" option that enables you to apply for jobs during your spare time throughout the day. With this one tool, you can continue your job search anytime and anywhere.

While broad market job boards are good, they are by definition not specific or non-targeted. Many employers know that when they post a job to a broad market job board they will get hundreds of resumes that may include less qualified candidates. For this reason, companies often only post jobs on industry specific job boards. Since these job boards are only known within specific industries and disciplines, they tend to provide employers with fewer and more qualified candidates. If you are not sure which would be the right industry specific job board, just do a Google search like "tech job listings". The first organic search result for this activity is Dice.com. I really like Dice.com for technology and IT jobs. Beware that some broad industry job boards, like Indeed or Monster, may try to advertise in Google that they are an industry specific job board...don't be fooled. While they do list many IT and technology jobs, they are broad market job boards. Do your homework and find the best or most popular job board for your industry. The chances are, you have never heard of it.

A third type of job board to target are skill or job specific job boards. Start your research by doing a Google search. For example, if you search "Auto Mechanic job board" you will find http://www.Needtechs.com as a job board specifically for automotive mechanics and technicians. Once you have found the right job board, create your profile, setup job alerts, and start applying for your target job title.

6. Trade and industry associations

These days it seems like every job has some type of trade or industry association representing it and running trade shows. These associations typically have websites that include a career section with highly targeted jobs for your industry and skill. Start by doing a Google search. For example, if you search for "nurses' association" you will find the American Nurses Association or AMA, along with many different nursing associations. The AMA has a career center that functions just like an online job board. You can create your profile, set up alerts for your target job, and start applying directly from there.

7. Consulting Firms

For those professionals who excelled in college, you may consider working with a consulting firm. Consulting firms typically offer their services to Fortune 500 companies in specific industries, such as: defense, economy, energy, health care, human resources, IT operations, IT strategy, management, operations, public sector, retail, and strategy. Many of these firms seek out skilled professionals that excelled in college and have Fortune 500 work experience. These jobs typically pay high salaries and require that you frequently travel to the customer's work location. These jobs aren't for everyone, but many candidates find consulting to be an excellent career path.

8. Entrepreneur

If you are a professional with an entrepreneurial sales background, you might want to start your own Sales Consulting or Manufacturer's Agent business. This gives you the flexibility to supplement your income and work with companies and customers with which you may have existing relationships. Go to the http://RepHunter.net or The Manufacturing Agents National Association websites for more information.

Some people find that this time in their career is the right time to go it alone and create their own business. Creating a business has many benefits, but it also involves high risk. Before jumping into your own business and spending your precious nest-egg, I recommend that you consult with your Trusted Advisor and seek advice from non-profit organizations such as SCORE (http://www.Score.org). SCORE connects entrepreneurs with mentors to help them build a business with free business advice. These organizations can help you put the right business plan together and avoid many of the common pitfalls of starting a small business.

9. Freelance

For some professionals, working for a company is no longer their goal. Becoming a freelance professional can offer many benefits without the hassles of working for someone else. Find the freelance job board that best fits your skill and create a professional profile and business offering. Try well-known freelance job boards, such as Upwork/Elance, Toptal, Freelancer, Craigslist, and Guru.

Step 7: Prepare for the Phone Screen

Now it's time to prepare for the phone screening. The chances are high that you will receive a phone call at some inopportune time. Consider this phone call as you would an interview, because the recruiter or manager will make decisions based upon how and what you communicate during the call. If you are in a noisy environment, move to somewhere quiet or ask to call them back at a better time, in a few minutes or later that day. However, make sure to call them back that day. If you don't, it sends the impression that you aren't serious or interested.

The initial phone screening is to ascertain if you are the person you represent yourself to be on your resume, and to get a feel for your skills and personality. It is important that you have done all your research on your target job title and are comfortable talking about how your experience applies to the job at hand. You will be asked about your resume, prior work experience, and education. Make sure that you can quickly and easily recall this information and present it in a positive light.

During the screening, it is important to put your best foot forward and communicate only what you feel will reflect positively on you as a candidate. Don't think that just because it's a phone call with a person you have never met, it is not important that you articulate yourself well. Avoid typical pitfalls during the phone screening, such as giving long responses to questions, bad mouthing a prior employer, or being slow or unprepared to answer questions about your resume, experience, or education. Know your resume well enough that you can have a totally natural and relaxed conversation. Stay cool and don't allow yourself to be overly stressed. Interviewers know that candidates will be nervous during a call or interview. This is normal, but if you allow your stress to interfere with the way you communicate, that is a red flag. Employers expect employees to be able to cope with stress as part of everyday work.

Some phone screenings will be scheduled so you have time to prepare. If this is the case, spend some time reviewing the company's website and become familiar with their business, brands, and products. This will help you to be better prepared and provide the best answers to the phone screening questions. For example, if all your answers reflect your experience in a different industry, that may be adequate, but the best answers would reflect your experience put in the context of the hiring company's industry.

During the phone screen, it is not uncommon for the recruiter to ask, "What are your salary requirements?" This is a very normal question for people that work as contractors. If you are unfamiliar or unprepared to discuss the topic, just ask the recruiter what the allocated budget is for that position. They will typically volunteer this information, since they don't want to waste their time or yours. If they find a good candidate that has higher salary requirements than the job requisition, they want to know that right away so they can move on to the next candidate. Their time is valuable, so expect them to be very efficient, business-like, and objective. Before the phone screening, you should already have a good idea of what the job pays by going to sites like Salary (http://www.Salary.com) or Glassdoor (http://www.Glassdoor.com) and review average salaries for your target job.

At the end of the phone screen, don't forget to ask what the interviewer's next steps and timeline will be. Get permission to follow up with them at a pre-determined date so you leave nothing to chance. Don't forget to get the person's contact information before the end of the call.

Video Phone Screen

To improve the screening process, many companies and recruiters now conduct a live screening by using video conferencing. A live video screening gives the employer the opportunity to see you and how you present yourself. It is important that you dress at an appropriate level for this interview. I would suggest business casual or a suit and tie depending on the opportunity. Prepare for the phone screening as you would a face-to-face interview and ensure that you are well-groomed.

Conducting a video screening, requires that you have a modern computing device such as a smartphone, tablet, notebook, or desktop computer with an operating microphone and video camera. Most companies use tools such as Skype (https://www.Skype.com) to host the meeting. If the interviewer requests a video screening, you should prepare and test your ability to attend the video screening at least one day before the meeting, and verify that you are using the correct service.

These steps include:

- Confirm your device has a microphone and video camera.
- Download the application from the Apple or Android App Store or go to the website of the service the interviewer uses and download the app.
- Test the app by hosting your own video conference with a friend or family member. Make sure the video and audio quality is excellent and it is easy for both of you to understand each other.
- As part of the test, verify that you are on a network that provides reliable high speed internet connectivity even during peak hours.
- Do not plan to attend the video call in a public location, such as a restaurant or coffee shop, since you have no control over the environment and noise level.
- If you do not have a suitable location for the interview, ask someone you know if you can use their home or office or request that the screening occur without video.

Appropriate Follow up

After the phone screening is complete, it is perfectly normal to send an email to the interviewer thanking them for their time and briefly highlighting why you are excited about the opportunity. This email should be short and to the point. If you are long winded, you will begin to sound desperate and that will lower your chances of getting invited to interview face to face. You want to be polite, gracious, and pithy.

Step 8: Prepare for the Interview

Purpose

Congratulations! The phone screening went well and you have received an invitation for a face-to-face interview. There are several things to keep in mind to set the right expectation. First, you are probably one of several candidates being invited to interview. Second, every candidate will most likely be qualified to perform the job duties. Third, managers are busy people with many responsibilities so their time is valuable. They will only interview candidates that they think can perform the job so the interview is to determine if you fit the job, the team, and the company. The interview is to determine if they like you, and a job offer will come down to the hiring managers' gut feelings with input from the team that may have helped interview you. Some hiring managers use complex questions and scoring methods, but at the end of the day, it's a gut decision.

What to expect

There is no standard interview process. Every company and person conducts an interview differently based upon their perspective, goals, and experience. Even when a company has a formal interview process, the individual interviewers are free to "do their own thing" when it comes down to the actual interview. For these reasons, there is no one set method for preparing for an interview, but there are some techniques that will help you put your best foot forward. Some interviewers will ask standard questions, such as "what are your top three strengths and weaknesses?" Some companies use a technique called Behavioral Interviewing, which requires you to think back on your experience and give specific examples of work or situations. Other companies try to be creative and/or technical, and give you puzzles or word games to understand how you approach problem solving.

Pre-Work and Study

Putting effort into preparing for an interview is just as important as the effort and time you spent planning and writing your resume. I would recommend that you spend at least 2 hours preparing for an interview. Preparation should include: 1) studying the interviewing company, employees, industry, and competitors 2) studying your resume so you know it inside and out 3) creating, answering, and practicing your responses to some of the most popular interview questions.

It is important to study the interviewing company for many reasons, and these include the certainty that the interviewer will ask how familiar you are with the company. From an interviewer's perspective, they want to know so they can ask the most appropriate questions. From your perspective, you want to know so you can have as natural and relaxed a conversation as possible. If you haven't done your research, they will quickly see that you aren't prepared, and that may put you at a disadvantage when a hiring decision is made.

One technique that can be extremely helpful is to spend some time reviewing each interviewers' LinkedIn profile. Reviewing their profile helps you understand who they are, what they have done, where they went to school, and how much education they have. This gives you an idea on what type of person they are and how to approach them during the interview. For example, you may find that you both attended the same school, worked at the same prior employer, or both follow the same sports team. The first few minutes of a face-to-face interview is a crucial time for you to introduce yourself, build rapport, and gain trust.

Once you understand who you will be meeting with, use the company website and Google Finance to review the company profile and industry. When you have an understanding of the company, their goals, financial position and culture, you will be in a position to respond to interview questions with a better understanding of where the interviewer is coming from. I have been in interviews where some of my answers didn't seem to satisfy the interviewer. This can happen very easily if your experience is not well-aligned to the employer's industry. It feels to the interviewer that you aren't a great fit because you "just don't get it". This is what I mean by the gut feel decision to hire a candidate. If a candidate doesn't look like a duck, sound like a duck, and act like a duck, they must not be a duck. You want to make yourself look, sound, and act like you have spent years in the metaphorical trenches with the interviewer. You will only achieve this comfort level and confidence through study and preparation.

Imagine for a moment of being a hiring manager and having an interview candidate sit down in front of you that not only understands your products, company, and culture but also understands your competitors. If you want to sell yourself as the best fit for the job, going the extra mile to review each competitor and recent press releases on Google Finance could give you the edge you need to walk away with a great offer.

If you prepare well and have educated questions for the interviewer, it achieves several positive goals. Firstly, it shows the employer that you have done your due diligence and really want the job. It also gives you something in common to discuss, which relaxes both parties and builds rapport and trust. Another positive is that the time you take asking insightful questions could reduce the amount of time that the interviewer would use to ask *you* questions. Finally, it allows the interviewer to spend time talking about what they care about, which often makes the interviewer feel better about the outcome of the interview. Generally, the more you can get the interviewer to talk and share about their company, the better the interview goes.

Use Table 7 to review the company, industry, and competitor's information online as part of your interview preparation.

Behavioral Interviewing Techniques

Let me take a few minutes to help you prepare for an interviewer that may use a popular method called Behavioral Interviewing. Behavioral Interviewing works off the philosophy that a candidate's prior experience is the best indicator of their future success. The technique is designed to ask questions that force the candidate to think of and share specific examples in their past which demonstrate the core skills and/or abilities required for success in the new job. An example would be, "Tell me about a time when you had an interpersonal conflict with a team member or co-worker". Some follow up questions provide further understanding as follows: "What methods or techniques did you use to resolve the conflict?", "Was it successful or not?", and "What did you learn from the experience?"

Behavioral Interviewing can be exhausting for a candidate that has not prepared for this technique. When I interviewed at Intel, I spent all day with several different interviewers asking me Behavioral Interviewing questions. I left completely exhausted and brain dead!

Before answering any interview question, take a moment to think about what was asked and consider your answer before blurting out the first thing that comes to mind. If you didn't understand the question, ask the interviewer to repeat the question. Remember, taking a few extra moments to think of your best example is normal. Interviewers understand they are asking about something that may have happened several years ago, so slow down, relax, and provide your best examples.

One method you can use to prepare and practice your answers, is to review a list of popular questions and prepare your responses using the STAR method. STAR is an acronym for Situation, Task, Action, and Results.

- **Situation** - describe the background or context of the situation.
- **Task** - describe the Task and expectations for what was being accomplished.
- **Action** - describe what you did, how you did it, and what tools you used.
- **Results** - describe the result, accomplishments or recognition you or the team received for completing the task.

Use Table 9 to write down a few short answers to some popular types of Behavioral questions. These questions are only generic examples. I would expect that the interviewer will tailor the question to the specific industry and skillset required for the job at hand.

Table 10: Sample Behavioral Interview Questions

Sample Questions	Abbreviated Answers
Interpersonal Skills: Tell me about a time when you had an interpersonal conflict with a team member or co-worker. What methods or techniques did you use to resolve the conflict? Was it successful or not? What did you learn from the experience?	Situation: Task: Action: Results:
Coping Ability: Please share a time when you were under a great deal of stress at work. What did you do to cope? Were your coping methods successful?	Situation: Task: Action: Results:
Challenges and Failure: Can you tell me about a time when a project you worked on failed? Why did it fail? What actions did you take for corrective action? Did you or the team communicate risks and/or issues early and often? What was the outcome or result? What would you do different on your next project?	Situation: Task: Action: Results:
Leadership: Please share with me a time when you took a leadership role on your team. What did you do to prepare? What challenges did you overcome? How did you rally the team around a goal?	Situation: Task: Action: Results:
Problem Solving: Tell me about the time when you had a complex problem to solve. How did you approach the problem? What tools did you use? What was the outcome?	Situation: Task: Action: Results:
Teamwork: Please share a time when you participated on a "high performance team". What were the core characteristics of the team? How did the team govern itself? How did the team handle change? What did the team achieve?	Situation: Task: Action: Results:
Complexity: Please share with me the most challenging book that you have ever read. What made it challenging? Did it change your perspective?	Situation: Task: Action: Results:

THE INTERVIEW

You have planned, studied, practiced, and prepared for the Interview and the big day is finally here. Following are a few things to consider for the Interview process. First, let's set expectations. If you are asked to attend a face-to-face interview, expect that you are one of three to eight people that have been invited to interview for the same job. Each person will technically qualify for the job, so it is your job to sell yourself and show them how you will help their organization achieve their goals.

Bring several copies of your formatted resume on heavy quality paper in a presentable folder. Most interviewers will only have a text based printout from the HR database, so getting a nice formatted resume in their hands is crucial to making a great first impression.

The guidelines for clothing and grooming is to wear at least one step above what you expect the company dress code to be. Wearing a suit and tie or a modest dress to an interview is almost never a bad idea, unless it's a surf shop on Hermosa Beach. In those cases, use your good judgement not to overdress. For recent college graduates, the concept of going to the dry cleaner may be new to you. Take the time now to start a habit of having neatly pressed shirts, pants, or dresses for work. How you dress communicates a great deal about you and your aspirations. As they say, "dress to impress" or even better, "dress for the job you want". If you are poorly dressed or wear shabby clothes, it usually does not give a positive impression. Drop off your interview clothes at the dry cleaners' several days before the interview, so there is one less thing to worry about. Ensure that your shoes are clean and polished. A wise man once said, "I can tell all I need to know about a man from his shoes". Whether you know how to polish shoes or not, don't let yourself be undone by the details. It matters.

On the subject of grooming, it never hurts to be clean shaven and neatly groomed. As times change, acceptable grooming standards also change, so use good judgement, but know that being conservative almost never back-fires. On the other hand, having long hair or visible tattoos may put your job offer at risk. Once again, depending on the job and industry, use your good judgement. The idea is to minimize any negatives the interviewer may perceive because when it comes down to the final gut check, it may be the deciding factor.

Plan to arrive at the interview location with plenty of time available to address potential traffic problems and to find the building and parking. Being early or punctual is always good. Being late is unacceptable.

Once the interview starts, introduce yourself with confidence. Provide a firm hand shake and make direct eye contact with the interviewer. Do not wear sunglasses.

The formal interview comes down to a sales presentation. You are selling your most prized commodity, yourself. Knowing that this commodity is very valuable, how would you go about selling it to a buyer? Rookie salespeople often pull out brochures or models to convince the buyer of the product's amazing features and value. I have found that you can spend all day selling someone on a feature or benefit, but ultimately what makes them purchase is whether they like you. If the buyer doesn't like the salesman, he will go out of his way to buy from somebody else. For the most important sale of your life, what is the key thing you need to achieve in the interview? It is certainly not telling the interviewer how your superior skills will make them millions. It is not telling them how your abilities are beyond every other candidate they will meet. The art of the deal is to build as much rapport, trust, and likeability as you can in the few minutes you have with this stranger. The goal is to get the interviewer to like and trust you more than any other candidate, because we all know, any of the candidates can do the job. In addition, if you think you are not a people person or not good at meeting people, that doesn't matter. This is what you *must* do to land the job. Here are a few steps to help you build rapport, likeability, and trust.

First is the warm-up. The warm-up is the first few minutes of any interpersonal interaction. The warm-up includes introducing yourself, making direct eye contact, smiling, and sharing a warm and heartfelt salutation. This instantly sets the tone for a positive engagement.

When I was in financial sales, the warm-up started when I first pulled in front of the client's house. I would scan everything about the neighborhood, the street, the house, the front door, the paint, entry way, and interior of the house. I would attempt to learn as much about the client as I could, and fill my war chest of conversation topics for a thorough warm-up. By paying attention to the surroundings, you will find things of interest to talk about, for example, sports, family, beliefs, etc. A successful warm-up ends when you leave the meeting. Some of the most successful sales people spend the entire meeting making small-talk and don't get to the point until the last few minutes of the meeting. This used to drive me crazy! However, I learned that by taking the time to get to know the client, or interviewer, in this situation, you show interest, build trust, and become much more likeable than any other candidate.

I have heard stories of some of the best salespeople spending the entire hour in the warm-up, then in the last few minutes closing a deal worth hundreds of thousands of dollars. Since the client trusted the salesperson, the details of the deal were a distant second priority to establishing a trusting relationship.

My recommendation is to start your warm-up by sharing things about yourself or things you may have in common with the interviewer. Some interviewers will resist the path you are trying to take and just want to ask you predetermined questions. If that's the case, follow along, but throughout the interview, take the time to share who you are, where you are from, and what you're about. When one person shares something personal, it normally compels the other person to share something about themselves as well.

As the interviewer gets into the groove of sharing about themselves, their likes, dislikes, family, hobbies, and company, they will become more and more comfortable with you as a person and will naturally like you more than the next candidate. I have practiced this technique, and it has surprised me how some interviewers will spend the best part of an hour talking about themselves and their company. By the time the interview ends, they come away thinking that it went really well, even though I said very little.

Second, be a good listener. Have you ever heard anybody complain that somebody was a good listener? Of course not. Being a good listener is so rare that it is considered a virtue. Being a good listener means that you genuinely care about wanting to understand the other person and what they are trying to communicate. Oftentimes we hear the first part of someone's statement, and our brains automatically jump ahead to our response. Active listeners discipline themselves to wait until the other person finishes their thought before even considering how to respond. When they do respond, they are thoughtful with the words and ideas they use. Most people are so used to being interrupted and not fully listened to that when they interact with someone that actively listens, they feel a deeper connection. This is exactly what you want to accomplish during the interview.

Third, smile and use humor. For hiring managers, interviewing multiple candidates is not the most fun thing in the world. If you conduct a good warm-up, actively listen, and throw in some humor, it makes the interview go smoothly and much more enjoyable for everyone. Many candidates find that the stress of interviewing and trying to be perfect makes it too hard to be funny. Unfortunately, this plays against you as a candidate. The more relaxed, happy, and fun you are, the more comfortable and trusting the interviewer will be. He or she will sense that you are having fun and aren't hiding anything. During the post interview review meeting, the interviewers will base their feedback on how they felt regarding your technical *and* behavioral skills. Assuming all candidates are qualified, your great behavioral skills will push you over the top and land you an offer.

SALARY

If the question of your salary requirements comes up, don't throw out a number you had in mind. Instead, ask the employer or recruiter what the employer has outlined as the budget for the requisition, or ask what they feel someone with your qualifications is worth in today's market. Assuming you *need* a job and don't have any leverage in this negotiation, go along with what is fair value. You should have a good idea what the job pays before going to the interview by reviewing salaries at http://www.Salary.com or http://www.Glassdoor.com.

SCARCITY

At the close of an interview or even during the initial phone screening, the recruiter or employer may ask if you have other interviews or offers on the table. The worst thing you can say to this question is no. It automatically places the thought in the hiring manager's mind, even at a subconscious level, that if nobody else has hired you, maybe there's a problem they aren't seeing. Instead, you want to respond in the affirmative that you have several opportunities that you are currently pursuing or interviews that are scheduled. By communicating in this way, you use the sales tactic of creating an environment of scarcity. This implies that you are in high demand and if the hiring manager doesn't make a decision soon, he may miss out on the opportunity to hire you. Your response provides the necessary stimulus to encourage the employer to make and communicate a decision to you as soon as possible. If you do receive an offer from multiple employers, feel free to communicate to those companies that you haven't yet made a decision, and give them the chance to counter offer. This will only work to your advantage.

Appropriate Follow up

Before you leave the interview, make sure to ask the hiring manager what his timeline is for making a hiring decision. Most hiring managers will be honest and forthright with their intentions. If they like you, they may even imply that you will receive an offer shortly, but most often they will hold back from making any firm commitments. An appropriate response to this is to ask if it is okay to follow up with them via a call or email after a week or so. Normally they will say yes or give you another contact. Some candidates are concerned that by contacting the hiring manager after the interview, they are potentially hurting their chances of getting the job. This is not the case. It is perfectly normal for the candidate to ask this question, not to mention it shows that you are the type of person that plans ahead and you are serious about the job.

After the interview, I suggest that you check in with all the interviewers over email with a short and concise "Thank you for taking the time to meet with me today. I enjoyed getting to know you and more about the position." You should avoid reinforcing why you are perfect for the job, as this may come off as desperate at this point.

Follow up with each employer weekly until you receive a definitive answer. I have personally received two job offers for the exact reason that I kept calling back and asking if a decision had been made, so don't give up too quickly. Once an employer tells you that you haven't been selected, thank them verbally or via email and disengage. It is important that you do this graciously and don't burn any bridges. You may have been the runner-up candidate, and employers oftentimes have new job openings or the other candidate may fall through or not work out. Be gracious, polite, and professional at all times.

Step 9: The Offer

Congratulations! You received an offer for employment! Before making any changes that will impact your life, make sure you get the offer in writing. The offer should include your job title, duties, start date, salary, bonus information, and a general statement about benefits. I had a situation in which an employer wanted to change my work location after I had already accepted the offer and made plans to move. If you don't get the offer in writing, the company is not legally obliged to compensate you for any expenses associated with a verbal offer. In my situation, it would have involved a massive change and expense as we were moving our home. Be sure to get it in writing!

Some companies do not provide a formal written job offer. In those instances, make sure you don't overextend yourself, in case things don't work out the first week. Typically, they will ask you to start on a specific day and come to a specific location.

Your acceptance of the offer can be written or verbal depending upon what the employer requires. For many companies, an offer of employment is contingent upon successfully completing a drug screening and background check, so don't count your chickens before they are hatched. If you have anything on your job application that would raise a red flag, like unreported felonies or false information, you may be at risk for immediate dismissal, even if you spend years working at the company. Your offer of employment is always contingent upon you providing accurate information. Intentionally misleading an employer by falsifying your job application is fraud, which is illegal. Unlike a marketing brochure, or resume, the job application is a legal document.

Step 10: Re-Plan

Dealing with Discouragement

Getting a full time job can be one of the hardest and most discouraging things you do in life. After months of diligently applying for hundreds of jobs, it is only natural for you to get discouraged and start to wonder if you have any value at all. Believe me, I've been there. During the Great Recession, I ended up in the job market, and it was miserable. After months of working all the angles, nothing seemed to come together, until finally, it happened.

For starters, having a Trusted Advisor to talk to will help you stay motivated and focus your efforts. Even after putting together a great plan and resume, you may still struggle to land a job for any number of reasons. The key to a successful job search is knowing that it will end, and probably sooner than it feels.

After applying to the same company several times, job seekers can get frustrated and feel that they are wasting their time. Keep in mind that large companies have thousands of employees and hundreds of different departments. Most job openings are not within the same department, so keep trying!

Another thing to consider is that you may have exhausted most of the job leads in your target geographic region. As your job search has taken longer than expected, your expectations may have also changed. You may have started your job search and created job board profiles and alerts for a narrow geographic region like your local city. As your job search and expectations evolve, take the time to go back and update your job search and alert profile on all the job boards you have used. Pay special attention to broadening the geographic search radius. This may present many new jobs that were previously beyond your radar.

Daily Checklist

A to-do list and daily checklist is included in the appendix to help you stay on track. Plan your day as though you are going to work. Find a quiet place with internet access and a computer, and then step through the checklist. I recommend getting up early to start work. Our brains learn, study, and retain information much better before lunch, so use these hours to be as effective as you can. Be consistent, disciplined, and most of all, patient with yourself.

Back To Step 3

After you have followed the daily checklist for several weeks, you may feel as though you could do more. If you feel you are equally qualified for several other target jobs, go back to Step 3 and plan your next strategy. Be patient, and create a solid plan and resume that appropriately targets a new target job. You may have the urge to create numerous targeted resumes. While I recommend this strategy, sometimes more is just more, and not more effective. Try to limit yourself to only three or four target jobs. Start with one, and master the daily process, then two, and then only add more if you can complete your daily checklist and respond to all job alerts for your highest priority target jobs.

Conclusion

In conclusion, you now have a plan and the tools necessary to secure an interview. For interview prep, take the time to practice interviewing with a friend or Trusted Advisor and say your responses out loud so you can get immediate aural feedback. Hearing your answers will help you improve with practice.

Gaining employment is a full time job, and it all comes down to putting the odds in your favor. Let me put things in perspective; the probability of getting a phone screening or interview right off the bat is low, likely in the 5-10% range. For this reason, you have to put the numbers on your side and make them work for you. To do this, make some educated assumptions about how much effort it will take based upon these odds. Let's assume it takes twenty online job applications to get one phone screening. Next, assume it takes ten phone screenings to get one face-to-face interview. Finally, assume it takes ten face-to-face interviews to get one job offer. Based on these numbers, it will take at least two hundred online job applications to get an offer of employment.

These numbers may even seem optimistic depending on the job market, geographic area, your resume, and skills. But if at first you don't succeed, continue working the program. Oftentimes something pops out of the blue when you least expect it.

Set the expectation early in your job search that the first few interviews will be for practice and to refine your pitch. After each interview, re-assess your situation and determine if you need to make a course correction in your plan. If you find that interviewers are asking for skills and/or experience you do not currently have, decide how to fill the gap, modify your approach and interviewing tactics, or re-plan around a new target job title.

Getting a great job is a full time job that requires planning, discipline and a positive attitude. To help keep you motivated and focused I have included a summary of the 10 step process and daily, weekly, and monthly checklists.

I hope that this workbook will help you on your way to a great and prosperous future. Good luck!

Appendix

10 Step To-Do List

- ☐ Step 1: Complete your self-assessment. Record your education and hard and soft skills. Identify a Trusted Advisor to help you through the process.
- ☐ Step 2: Conduct a job market analysis. Study broad market and career specific job boards to determine what jobs are in demand across different geographic regions.
- ☐ Step 3: Select the right career for you. Record your target job titles. Analyze and record industries, competitors, suppliers, and customers for your job search.
- ☐ Step 4: Create an SEO optimized and targeted resume. Write it from the perspective of your unique value and use qualities that are valued for your target job.
- ☐ Step 5: Create and/or update your online brand. Clean-up any social clutter or images online. Create a ninety percent complete LinkedIn profile and request recommendations.
- ☐ Step 6: Start applying for jobs.
- ☐ Step 7: Prepare for the phone screen. Practice out loud.
- ☐ Step 8: Prepare for the interview. Practice out loud. Review the sample behavioral interview questions and prepare your most appropriate and best answers.
- ☐ Step 9: Practice negotiating and accept the offer.
- ☐ Step 10: Re-plan based upon what you have learned and studied.

Sample Letter To Personal Contacts

John Doe

Address, City, State, Zip • 444-444-4444 • email@email.com

Date

Name
Company
Address
City, State Zip

Dear [Contact's Name]:

It has been a while since we last spoke and I hope all is well. I thought I would reach out to you as someone whose opinion I respect. I'm beginning a job search and thought it would be wise to get some differing perspectives on the job market prior to starting my campaign. That is when I thought of you.

As you may be aware, I left [Company] after [Number] years and joined [Company] as [Job Title] in order to expand my skills and experience. During my tenure, I successfully accomplished [Accomplishments] and that resulted in [Results].

Unfortunately, I was laid off due to company restructuring. Although it was sad to leave [Company, I am excited to find a new challenge.

I am seeking a position as [Desired Job Title], which will enable me to apply my [Relevant Skills] skills. Although I've worked primarily in the [Desired Industry] industry, I am open to most industries and will relocate for the right opportunity.

Any leads, ideas or advice regarding industries or companies that will help shorten my job search would be greatly appreciated. I will call you in a few days to follow up. Thanks in advance for the help. I look forward to speaking with you soon.

Thank you again for your time.

Sincerely,

Your Name

Sample Cover Letter

John Doe

Address, City, State, Zip • 444-444-4444 • email@email.com

To whom it may concern:

Are you looking to strengthen or rebuild your company's [Desired Department] department? [Provide a short summary of why you would add value to the prospective company.]

Please let me share some of the things that set me apart from other individuals:

- List a skill and/or quality you possess that is listed in the target job description

- List a skill and/or quality you possess that is listed in the target job description

- List a skill and/or quality you possess that is listed in the target job description

If my talents can assist you, please contact me at the number or email listed above.

Sincerely,

Your name

Sample Interview Thank You Letter

John Doe

Address, City, State, Zip • 444-444-4444 • email@email.com

Date

Name
Company
Address
City, State Zip

Dear [Interviewer's Name]:

Thank you for the time you spent with me discussing the position of [Job Title] for [company]. I really enjoyed meeting you and getting to know about the position and company.

Based upon our discussion, I am confident that I have the skills, experience, and personality that will enable me to do an excellent job. Here is why:

- List an area of concern with a short summary of how you can meet it (based upon what the employer needs)
- List an area of concern with a short summary of how you can meet it (based upon what the employer needs)

I look forward to speaking with you again to continue our discussion. As we agreed, I will be calling you on [Day of the Week and Date] if we have not spoken before then.

Thank you again for your time.

Sincerely,

Your Name

Sample References

John Doe

Address, City, State, Zip • 444-444-4444 • email@email.com

<u>REFERENCES</u>

Company Name:

- First Last, Title. Phone. Email
- First Last, Title. Phone. Email

Company Name:

- First Last, Title. Phone. Email
- First Last, Title. Phone. Email

Company Name:

- First Last, Title. Phone. Email
- First Last, Title. Phone. Email

The following section includes daily, weekly, and monthly checklists to help you stay focused and on track, once steps one through six are complete. Creating a daily routine will help make the work of finding a job more structured and methodical.

Daily Checklist (4-8 hours per day)

1. Review Google news business and finance sections during breakfast.
2. Follow up on leads from your personal network. Tailor your resume to each lead.
3. Review and apply to email leads from recruiters.
4. Review and apply to job board email alerts.
5. Review LinkedIn jobs where prior co-workers or friends may work.
6. Review and apply for jobs on career/industry or trade specific job boards.
7. Review and apply for jobs on broad market job boards.

Weekly Checklist (2-4 hours per week)

1. Follow up with your three targeted recruiting firms.
2. Follow up on phone screenings or interviews with the key contact.
3. Perform a Google search for job fairs or networking events in your area.
4. Schedule an informal lunch with a friend, mentor, or prior co-worker.

Monthly Checklist (1-2 hours per month)

1. Meet with your Trusted Advisor to review progress and make changes to your plan.
2. Expand your number of targeted recruiting firms by one or two.
3. Review your job board alert settings. Expand geographic search area.

Resources

Career Planning Support
Visit http://www.HowToGetAnOnlineJob.com for templates (resume, letters & references) and counseling support

Notes

_____

_____

_____

_____

_____

_____

_____

_____

_____

_____

_____

_____

_____

_____

_____

_____

_____

_____

_____

_____

_____

_____

_____

_____

ABOUT THE AUTHOR

Craig Britland is a first generation immigrant and fully naturalized citizen of the United States. Craig's family moved from the United Kingdom to Los Angeles, California in 1980. Craig's father, the late Keith Britland, followed a friend's advice and sacrificed a comfortable life to provide opportunity and a better life for his children.

Craig has been married to his high school sweetheart for over 25 years and has four children. He currently resides in Atlanta, Georgia and volunteers as a Boy Scout leader and Employment Specialist.

Craig holds degrees in Electronic Engineering Technology and Business Administration. Craig has worked in the following industries: Construction, Food Service, Hospitality, Finance, Electronics, Computer Hardware, Semiconductors, Information Technology, Software, Packaging, Automotive, and Insurance.

Career counseling services are available at:
http://www.HowToGetAnOnlineJob.com

Made in the USA
Charleston, SC
23 December 2016